To order additional copies of this book, contact:
Xlibris
1-888-795-4274
www.Xlibris.com
Orders@Xlibris.com

ISBN: Softcover   978-1-4797-7332-9
        Hardcover   978-1-4797-7333-6
        EBook   978-1-4797-7334-3

Library of Congress Control Number: 2012924364

Print information available on the last page.

Rev. date: 08/14/2019

Genois Wilson, FIREFIGHTER

She Dared to be First

by Carol Butler

Illustrated by Teresa Yarbrough

The author is grateful to:

Genois Wilson Brabson for sharing her story.

Teresa Yarbrough for sharing her talent and artistry
through beautiful illustrations.

Joan Bolden for sharing her impressions and the decision
she made as a young student.

Special thanks to the Fort Wayne Firefighters Museum and the
Fort Wayne Fire Department for their cooperation and support in
the making of this book.

This book is dedicated to my dear husband, **Tom;** my constant
source of encouragement, love and support.

Teresa Yarbrough, Genois Wilson Brabson, Carol Butler

Errrrrrrr, Errrrrrrr, Errrrrrrr!

The fire truck came screaming down East Wallace Street. Its siren was really loud. Where was it going? Whose house was on fire? All the children came running from their homes to see what the commotion was. The Number 2 Fire Station was only a few blocks away but the truck was moving very fast. Some of the firefighters were hanging on to the back of the truck as it sped down the street. The firefighters were ready to help the family whose home was on fire!

Genois Wilson was a little girl about eight years old. She played with all the children on East Wallace Street but her two best friends were Deloris and Janet. She knew that the sound of the siren meant one of her friends was in danger. She closed her eyes and said a prayer hoping all the children would be safe.

Genois and her family lived in the country outside a small town in Arkansas before they moved to Fort Wayne, Indiana.

When Genois was about a year old there was a fire in their home. Her sister was three years old. They were playing when her sister's dress caught on fire. The volunteers who came to fight the fire did not get to their home in time.

The fire burned her sister very badly. It was a very sad time for Genois and her family.

Genois and her family found a very busy city when they arrived in Fort Wayne, Indiana. There were many factories and businesses going strong. Men and women workers made TVs, trucks, wire used in electrical motors, and the very best potato chips – Seyfert's. Some workers were inventors. Their inventions helped Fort Wayne families and people around the world live better.

There were other jobs for people to do in the city, too. You could work downtown in a store, in an office, or become a nurse or teacher.

Some workers helped to keep everyone safe. They were police officers, firefighters, and deputies. When Genois was growing up most of the time only men could have these jobs.

Many African-American families came to Fort Wayne just like Genois and her family had. They were looking for better jobs and better schools for their children.

During the time Genois was growing up African-Americans were not allowed to live in every neighborhood and they were not allowed to have every job they wanted.

When a woman, man, girl or boy became the first African-American to do something or the first to be hired for a special job everyone was very, very proud.

From top, clockwise.

Toni Morrison, the first African-American woman to receive the Nobel Prize in Literature, she has also won the Pulitzer Prize for fiction.

Mae Jemison, the first African-American woman astronaut.

Hattie McDaniel, the first African-American woman to win an Oscar.

Shirley Chisholm, the first African-American woman elected to serve in the US Congress and the first African-American woman to run for President of the United States.

Genois decided she wanted to be a teacher when she grew up. She studied hard every year in school and while she was going to college she got a chance to work in a classroom assisting a teacher. Genois was glad that she got to learn what it would be like to be a teacher but she also believed there was something else she should be doing.

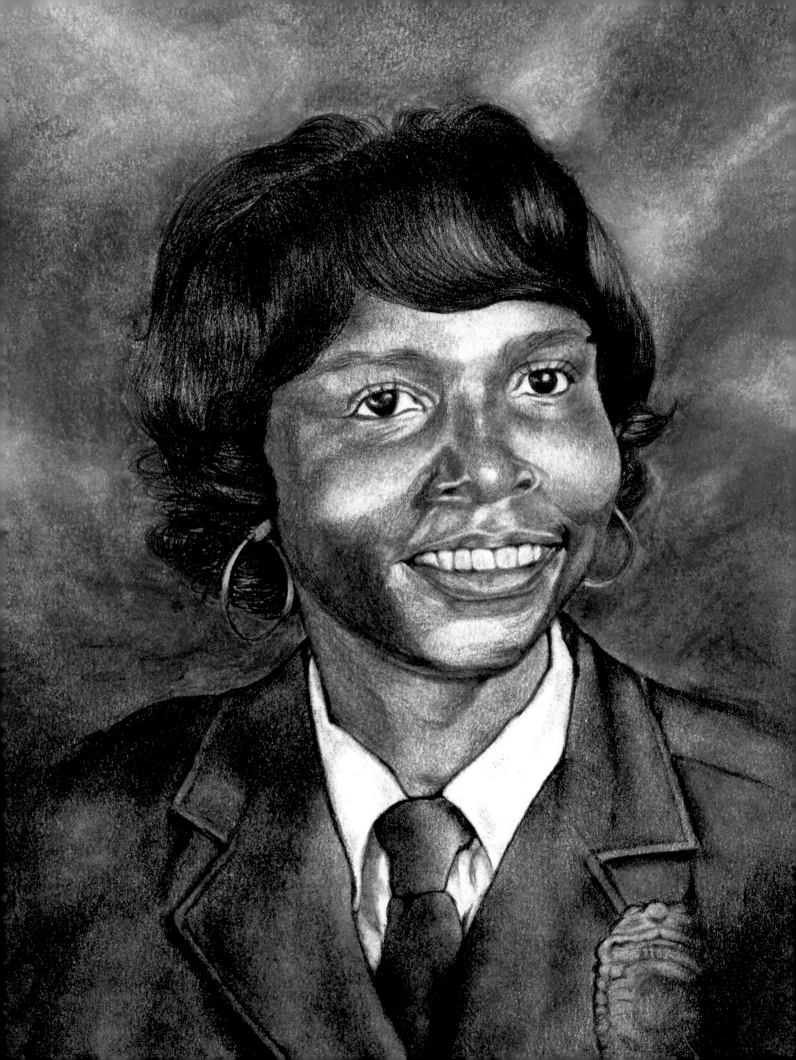

Genois started a new job working as the person who answered the calls for the Fire Department when people called for help. She sent the fire trucks to the offices, homes and buildings when there was a fire. It was a very important job. Then one day, Fire Chief Thomas Loraine asked if she wanted to make history and Genois said, "Yes!"

She started the Fire Department's training school and on March 30, 1975 Genois Wilson became the first woman firefighter in the Fire Department of Fort Wayne, Indiana!

It wasn't easy for Genois. She was the only woman. When the new firefighters were learning how to do their new jobs, she had to do everything the men did. She ran with them and lifted heavy weights and ropes like the ones used on the fire trucks. It was hard work but Genois was strong and determined and she passed the test.

The firefighters stayed at the fire station all day and all night. They were always ready to go if there was a fire. The male firefighters all slept together at the firehouse. But Genois could not stay with the men. She went home every night. It was many years before the fire department built rooms for women firefighters to stay overnight in the firehouse.

Then there was another change in Genois' life: she became a teacher just as she dreamed about. This time, she went to all the schools and she taught fire safety to hundreds of children.

Genois Wilson taught the schoolchildren how to use smoke detectors to save lives.

One day there was a big fire in a family's home. Because of the fire, everyone worked together. The firefighters, police, parents and teachers raised money to build the Survive Alive House at Safety Village. Children could now learn exactly what to do if they were in a fire.

Genois made sure everyone would have a smoke detector in their home. There were even smoke detectors for people who could not hear.

When Genois visited the schools she told the students about fire safety. They practiced things they should do if there was a fire drill at school or if the smoke detector went off during the night at their home.

Genois also told them how sad she was when she was with her sister and their home caught on fire. The children always listened to her and the fire safety lessons they learned from her saved many lives.

Genois followed her dream and made history when she said "Yes!" to Chief Thomas Loraine. She became the first woman firefighter in the city of Fort Wayne, Indiana.

She dared to be first. She worked hard and showed courage. She did very well in her career as a firefighter. She became a District Chief before she retired.

Many other women saw what Genois had done. They dared to follow in her footsteps and became firefighters. In 2012 the mayor of Fort Wayne named one of those women firefighters to be Chief of the Fort Wayne Fire Department.

Now,

What

Do

YOU

Dare

To

Dream?

Fort Wayne Fire Department Safety Tips

Featuring SADAR the Fire Dog!
SADAR's Tips for Kids

- "Stop, Drop, and Roll" if your clothes catch on fire.

- Stay away from "hot stuff" so your clothes never get burned.

- Never, ever play with fire. Fire is a tool, not a toy.

- Draw a home fire escape plan and practice it.

- If your home catches fire, "Stay Low and Go!"

- Never go back into a house that is on fire.

SADAR's Tips for Adults

- Do you know where your matches and lighters are?
- Do you have a smoke detector in every room of the house?
- Teach your children about fire and what to do.
- Use fire responsibly, practice what you teach!

Source: http://www.fortwaynefiredepartment.org/education/kids-page

Genois Wilson Brabson

When Genois Wilson Brabson graduated from the Fire Academy in the fall of 1979 her fellow recruits went to their assigned firehouses and she went to the Fire Department's Inspection Department. Her duties were to learn the local and state fire codes and inspect local businesses and public buildings. She also provided education to correct fire safety violations.

A crucial incident in Mrs. Wilson Brabson's career occurred in 1979 when a fatal house fire killed four siblings. Several of the children attended Lincoln Elementary school where she had done numerous fire safety presentations. The PTA and the school principal decided to help the fire department safety program by starting a fundraising program to make sure that no home would be without a smoke detector.

Genois credits her success to "the people in Fort Wayne; leaders who used their power well, the energy of parents and schools, the generosity of businesses, the Allen County Public Library and my Dad and Mom who taught me joy."

She and her husband, James, live in Fort Wayne, Indiana.

Teresa Yarbrough

Teresa is a greatly self-taught freelance artist. Born and raised in Fort Wayne, Indiana. She always loved art and seemed to have a natural talent for it. She was encouraged by teachers and particularly by supportive parents. Mother, Rosalind Ridley's artistic hand inspired her. Father, Richard Ridley Jr. provided, or even hand-made, any art tools she needed to succeed. Both taught her to believe that she could become anything she desired to be. This belief was reinforced by knowing her father helped shape history by being appointed Indiana's first African American firefighter and served with excellence.

Teresa, a US Air Force veteran, is trained in Commercial Art and Airbrush technique. She established, *'Heart & Soul Originals & Prints'* in January of 1992 marketing her work in California, Indiana & Las Vegas receiving exposure in media and print. She's hosted public displays and art shows, performed educational demonstrations for youth programs, and exhibited in galleries. Her virtual gallery is located at: *www.heartandsoularts.com*.

Teresa is a very diverse artist whose creations reflect a wide range of human interests including; aircraft nostalgic nose art, bigger than life murals, life-like portraits, artistic signage, to name a few. Children's book illustration is a new frontier this artist is embarking on with the first project so appropriately being, "Genois Wilson, Firefighter: She Dared to be First" about another historical first in the fire department of Fort Wayne, Indiana.

The artist's striking images, in this book, help to fill its pages with life and a fun visual experience for the children that read it!

Carol Butler is a community volunteer. She initiated Random Acts of Kindness Week; served as the chairperson of the International Women's Day planning committee, and is one of the founding members of an organization dedicated to supporting the university's Women's Studies program.

She is also an active member of the Baha'i Faith. Carol is married to Tom Butler and they live in Fort Wayne, Indiana. She and Tom love spending time with their grandchildren, travelling, and welcoming friends to their home.

Carol Butler was motivated to write this book about Genois Wilson, a woman who had dared to be first, because of a story a woman told her about being so influenced by Carol's visit to her high school as a young woman who had dared to be a Navy WAVE. Carol graduated from the U.S. Navy boot camp as a "Woman Accepted for Volunteer Emergency Service" or WAVE in April, 1968.

Joan Bolden, an employee at the Veterans Administration Medical Center greeted Carol one day. Joan told her when she was in junior high school she remembered Carol visiting her classroom wearing her WAVE uniform. As a young girl, Joan was so impressed by seeing Carol in uniform and the speech she gave that she decided right then to pursue a career in the Armed Forces. She served in two branches of the military: the U.S. Army and the Air Force.

Remembering Joan's story and believing that you can still change the world, "one child at a time" Mrs. Butler felt Genois Wilson Brabson's story needed to be and deserved to be told.

Printed in the United States
by Baker & Taylor Publisher Services

Printed in the United States
By Bookmasters